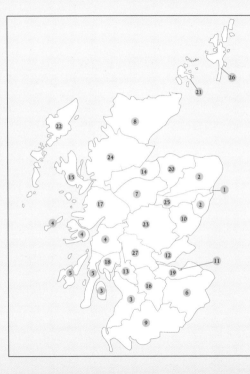

1. Aberdeen
2. Aberdeenshire
3. Arran & Ayrshire
4. Northern Argyll
5. Southern Argyll
6. The Borders
7. The Cairngorms
8. Caithness & Sutherland
9. Dumfries and Galloway
10. Dundee & Angus
11. Edinburgh
12. Fife, Kinross & Clackmannan
13. Glasgow
14. Inverness
17. Lochaber
18. Loch Lomond, Cowal & Bute
19. The Lothians
20. Moray
21. Orkney
22. The Outer Hebrides
23. Perthshire
24. Ross & Cromarty
25. Royal Deeside
26. Shetland
27. Stirling & The Trossachs

The remaining two books, Distinguished Distilleries and Scotland's Mountains, feature locations throughout the country so are not included in the above list.

2 Wideford Hill west of Kirkwall is a superb vantage point, especially to the north where many of Orkney's outer isles lie. This view shows Gairsay, Wyre, Rousay, Egilsay and, on the horizon, Westray.

ORKNEY

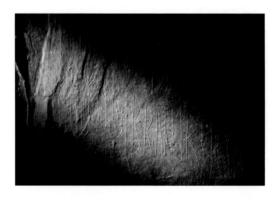

NESS PUBLISHING

ORKNEY

Welcome to Orkney!

A recurring TV advertisement for Scotland suggests that Scotland might surprise you. While that's true, it is also an understatement, as Scotland will frequently astonish you – and nowhere is that more true than in Orkney! Orkney is geologically spectacular, archaeologically unsurpassed (in Scotland), historically fascinating – and the food's not bad either! The pattern of islands that makes up Orkney begins about six miles north of Caithness on the Scottish mainland, separated from it by the frequently turbulent Pentland Firth. From southern tip to northernmost point is a straight-line distance of approximately 50 miles, but requires a journey by road and ferry of several hours. Going at a leisurely pace is part of the Orkney experience – hurry and you'll miss something crucial!

Given Orkney's history, the question of how Scottish it is bears asking. Before the Viking (or Norse) invasions that began around 800AD, it's clear that Orkney was part of the Pictish culture, like much of what would become Scotland, so there was common cause until then. But the Vikings' arrival led to Orkney becoming the epicentre of the great earldom of the Norse/Viking golden age. Orkney remained part of the Norse empire until 1468, so it has been Norse for longer than it has been part of Scotland!

Among Orkney's alumni of ancient sites, Skara Brae is the jewel in the crown and northern Europe's best-preserved Neolithic village. It is part of the Heart of Neolithic Orkney World

Sailing to Orkney from Scrabster provides a spectacular introduction to the islands thanks to the dramatic Hoy coast, the most notable feature of which is the 137m/449ft Old Man of Hoy.

Heritage Site, which also includes Maeshowe, the Stones of Stenness and the Ring of Brodgar. And, as if those treasures weren't enough, since 2002 they have been joined by the excavations at the Ness of Brodgar where discoveries of 'seismic' significance have been unearthed. Year by year as the dig progresses, the finds there are modifying and illuminating our understanding of Neolithic society in Orkney to an unprecedented degree.

Orkney has played a pivotal role in the defence of the British Isles. The huge haven of Scapa Flow has provided safe anchorage for ships for centuries. The British Navy based scores of vessels there in both World Wars. In 1939 *HMS Royal Oak* was torpedoed by a German U-boat and sank with the loss of over 800 lives. To limit the possibility of this happening again, Winston Churchill ordered that barriers be constructed between the islands on the eastern side of Scapa Flow. Once built, the four barriers effectively created land bridges that connected the islands of Lamb's Holm, Glimp's Holm, Burray and South

6 A look through the covered connecting passageway between houses at Skara Brae. See also pp.8-9 and 26-27.

Ronaldsay, which greatly eased travel in this part of Orkney. Today's road crosses the barriers (see pp.84-85). 60,000 personnel were stationed in Orkney during the Second World War.

This book is arranged in the form of a journey around Orkney that begins and ends with what approaching (and departing) travellers see from the Scrabster to Stromness ferry. As Stromness is situated on the western edge of Orkney's Mainland, it is a good point from which to begin a broadly circular tour which will take in most of the 17 inhabited islands (there are 67 in all). On the way we shall encounter an astonishing density of ancient sites from the Neolithic, Bronze and Iron Ages, coastal scenery that tests the credulity in its often gravity-defying qualities and pastoral vistas that sooth the senses. If those attributes were not enough, add in a charming capital with magnificent cathedral, a wealth of wildlife that will entrance nature lovers and a huge array of defensive remnants from both world wars. Do enjoy the tour!

Two of the tallest remaining stones at the henge monument of the Stones of Stenness. 7
See also pp.16-17.

8   Skara Brae Neolithic Village today stands right on the shore of the Bay of Skaill, as the picture shows. But when the village was occupied, it was some distance from the sea. Although the current

setting makes a picturesque scene, coastal erosion has made the village vulnerable to storm damage, with boulders and seaweed quite often being hurled upon it by stormy seas.

10 Picking up the trail of the journey begun on p.5, our point of arrival in Orkney is the town of Stromness. This view from the ferry shows some of the ancient jetties that line the shore.

This house belonged to Alexander Graham who, from 1743, led local merchants to oppose their tax **11** liability to the Royal Burgh of Kirkwall, resulting in Stromness becoming an independent burgh.

12 These two pictures show examples of the many wynds (lanes) that climb up the hillside on one side of the main street and drop down to the sea on the other, all part of Stromness' charm.

Stromness in snow. The town's main period of growth began in 1670 when chosen by the Hudson 13
Bay Company as the first and last port-of-call for their ships en route to and from Canada.

14 A few miles east of Stromness, Maeshowe's mound hides a masterpiece of ancient engineering: a chambered tomb constructed 5,000 years ago. At midwinter the setting sun shines right through

the entrance passage and illuminates this central chamber. About 1,000 years ago, Norsemen broke
in and left their mark – literally – in the form of many runic inscriptions – see p.1.

16 Only about a mile to the north, these are the largest three of the remaining monoliths at the
Stones of Stenness. This circle and henge monument dates to around 3000BC. Clearly a ritual site,

what is less clear is just what the form and purpose of those rituals were. However, the interpretation **17**
of its purpose may be furthered by ongoing discoveries at nearby Ness of Brodgar.

18 Close to the Stones of Stenness (see right of picture) is Barnhouse Neolithic village where the remains of 12 houses have been discovered so far, three of which can be seen here.

Currently, the area of greatest archaeological excitement is at the Neolithic complex discovered **19** at the Ness of Brodgar, the narrow isthmus between the lochs of Stenness and Harray.

20 Just north of Ness of Brodgar is Orkney's largest stone circle, the Ring of Brodgar. This huge henge monument is 104m/340ft in diameter and originally comprised about 60 stones, 27 of which remain

standing today, with a further nine fallen stones in evidence. The site is Neolithic, perhaps slightly younger than the Stones of Stenness but that is not proven. See also the front cover.

22 Corrigall Farm Museum at Harray portrays a typical Orkney farmhouse and steading as it would have been in the mid to late 19th century, complete with peat fire.

Moving across to the west coast of Orkney's Mainland, here is one of the more mind-boggling sea stacks. Named Yesnaby Castle, the probability of it lasting much longer seems slim . . .

24 Orkney also has its gentler side. This lovely pastoral scene is only a few miles inland from the rugged Yesnaby coastline, yet we could be in another country. Orkney is in fact predominantly

an agricultural landscape with the emphasis on livestock farming, as growing crops this far north is 25
a marginal exercise. However, hay is plentiful, with a recently cut field in the middle of the picture.

26 Returning now to Skara Brae, this is the wonderfully preserved interior of house no.1. The hearth is in the middle of the floor, with box beds to its left and an elaborate dresser faces the entrance.

Ten houses survive at Skara Brae, these being nos. 4 and 5. The village was continuously inhabited for some 600 years from about 3100BC to 2500BC, after which it became buried in sand dunes. **27**

28 Kirbister Farm is another of Orkney's museums that re-creates island life in times past. This room is an early 18th-century 'firehoose', with the smoke going through an opening in the roof.

Further north, up the west coast from Skara Brae, is Marwick Head. The tower is the memorial to **29** Lord Kitchener, Britain's WW1 Commander-in-Chief whose ship was sunk near here in June 1916.

30 The Brough of Birsay, a tidal island on Orkney's north coast, was an important settlement in the Pictish era of the 7th and 8th centuries and then for the Vikings. Inset: fulmars in conversation!

Norsemen began to settle in the 9th century and developed the village over the next 300 years, **31** the final phase of which included a Romanesque church, seen on the right of the picture.

32 Question: is the prone man near the cliff edge aware just how much it is undercut? Right: the Brough of Birsay is a haven and nesting place for several species of seabirds including many puffins.

Back on the mainland in the village of Birsay stand the gaunt but substantial ruins of the **33** Earl's Palace, built by Robert Stuart, Earl of Orkney, in the late 16th century.

34 Following the coast road round the east side of Mainland brings us to the Broch of Gurness. This Iron Age settlement comprised a mighty central broch tower surrounded by a small village.

On the opposite side from the previous picture, this is the most impressive broch entrance in **35** Orkney. The stone courses in the foreground are the bases of what was once a defensible gateway.

36 Across Eynhallow Sound on the island of Rousay is the equally well-preserved Midhowe Broch. Broch towers were complex structures standing up to 12-14m/39-46ft high and utilising

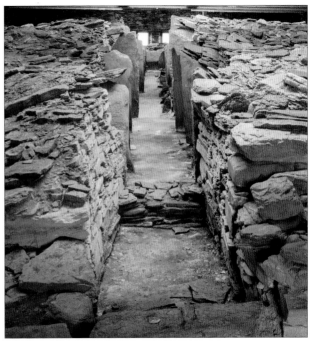

double-walled construction, joined in places for extra strength as shown above. Right: close by, Midhowe Cairn is a huge and impressive megalithic chambered tomb of Neolithic date, with 12 stalls.

38 A circuit of Rousay, Orkney's hilliest island after Hoy, reveals a blend of scenery both pastoral and rugged. This view across Saviskaill Bay is backed by the cliffs of Faraclett Head.

Lying just off the east coast of Rousay, the island of Egilsay is home to the complete but roofless ruin **39** of 12th-century St Magnus Church, located on the spot where Magnus was martyred.

40 Pausing to enjoy moments like this is another part of the Orkney experience. Scattered clouds are being under-lit by the setting sun, adding nature's pyrotechnics to the end of a fine day on the

island of Sanday, which will be explored on pp.56-61.

42 Left: moving on to the island of Wyre, the tranquil remains of St Mary's Chapel show off this pair of Romanesque arches. Right: moat detail at nearby Cubbie Roo's Castle, built around 1145.

The next port of call is Balfour on the isle of Shapinsay, a 25-minute crossing from Kirkwall. **43**
For a long period in the 18th and 19th centuries, Shapinsay was the domain of the Balfour family.

44 They carried out a programme of agricultural modernisation in the 1800s. The island remains intensively farmed. They also built Balfour Castle, above, which was completed in 1848.

Left: the Douche, a salt-water shower topped with a dovecot, is located near the harbour which can **45** be seen in the background. Right: Elwick water mill, situated on the edge of Balfour village.

46 And so from Shapinsay (just visible on the top right horizon) we arrive in Orkney's capital, Kirkwall, with this bird's-eye view from the tower of St Magnus Cathedral. Much of today's town is built on

reclaimed land – the shore line used to be right in front of St Magnus Cathedral. The row of buildings running from the left of the picture therefore marks where the reclamation began.

48 St Magnus Cathedral has stood in Kirkwall for more than 800 years. Building began in 1137 under Rognvald, nephew of St Magnus. This east-end view shows off the lovely colour of the sandstone.

A visit to St Magnus Cathedral is greatly enhanced by taking the Upper Levels tour from which **49** spectacular views like this (the nave towards the west window) can be enjoyed.

50 Left: the magnificent west window, unveiled by Her Majesty The Queen in 1987, deserves this closer inspection. Right: looking down to the choir from the triforium.

The north aisle of St Magnus Cathedral seen during the annual flower festival. The statue on the left **51** is of St Olaf, founder of the original Norse church that gave the name 'Church Bay' to Kirkwall.

52 Across the road to the south of the cathedral is the Bishop's Palace, one of the oldest surviving fortified residences in Scotland. Hakon IV of Norway died here in 1263 following the battle of Largs.

Next to the Bishop's Palace is the Earl's Palace, built by Earl Patrick Stuart c. 1600. It has been **53** described as 'possibly the most accomplished piece of Renaissance architecture left in Scotland'.

54 Tankerness House goes back to 1574, beginning life as a cathedral property built for the Archdeacon of St Magnus Cathedral. Today it houses the excellent Orkney Museum.

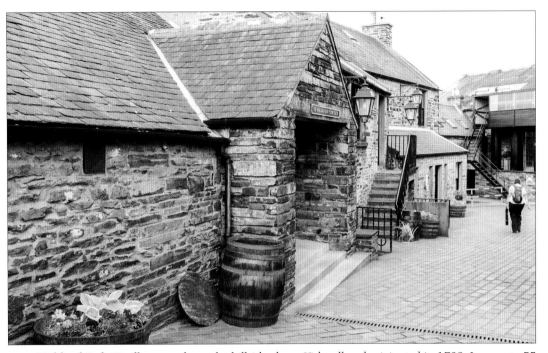

Highland Park Distillery stands on the hillside above Kirkwall and originated in 1798. In recent **55** years it has twice won the accolade of 'Best Spirit in the World'. This is the Visitor Centre.

56 After the bustle of Kirkwall it's time to get to know Orkney's northern isles, where the pace can be a little different. The largest of these is Sanday, often referred to as 'sunny Sanday' and, as this

picture shows, it often lives up to the name. While beautiful beaches abound in Orkney, this one at **57** Whitemill Bay on Sanday's north coast is particularly fine.

58 Over on the southern coast at Els Ness stands the somewhat fortress-like Quoyness chambered cairn. It is approximately contemporary with Maeshowe and, internally, there are similarities.

Start Point is the most easterly tip of Sanday and location of this 1806-built lighthouse which must **59** be as conspicuous by day as by night! It was Scotland's first revolving light.

60 Sanday has suffered serious de-population, from 2,000 in 1881 to 478 in 2001. However, there has been a slight increase since then. Perhaps the wild flowers are helping to draw people in.

Sanday is low-lying and looks vulnerable to the sea in a view like this. Looking across Backaskaill **61** Bay, the village of Kettletoft sits on the nearer promontory and the further one is Els Ness.

62 The next crossing is south to Stronsay. On a day of sunshine and showers, the ferry *Varagen* arrives at the port of Whitehall, a herring-boom village which therefore goes back to the early 1800s.

Once again, coastal erosion makes an impressive sight. This feature is known as the Vat of Kirbuster. **63**
Inset: like so many parts of Orkney, Stronsay is rich in bird life: this shag poses patiently.

64 As previously mentioned, stormy seas are a frequent threat to the low-lying parts of Orkney, of which there are many. Here on Stronsay's east coast, the waves pound in spectacular fashion.

The boom-time may be long gone, but Whitehall still supports a number of fishing boats, as these **65** fish crates testify. From here it's a short crossing westward to Eday.

66 One of Eday's important ancient sites is the Stone of Setter which, at 4.5m/15ft high, is arguably the finest prehistoric single standing stone in Orkney. It overlooks the Bay of Calf Sound.

17th-century Carrick House stands on the shore of the Bay of Calf Sound, with the hills of Red **67** Head rising beyond. On a clear day you can see Fair Isle (see *Picturing Scotland: Shetland*) from there.

68 Eday has several chambered tombs, one of which is on Vinquoy Hill. The rocks in the foreground may mark where the tomb's stones were quarried. Inset: the interior of Vinquoy Hill tomb.

And this is Eday in winter mood – those geese must have cold feet! Mainland Orkney is in the distance. We now bid Eday farewell and cross the Sound of Faray to reach Westray.

70 The ferry docks here in Rapness Sound, so this is the first sight of Westray that many visitors have of the island that is known as the 'Queen o' the Isles'.

Situated in the north of Westray, Noltland Castle is an incomplete Z-plan fortress built in the 16th century by Mary, Queen of Scots' Sheriff of Orkney, Gilbert Balfour.

72 Westray has its share of coastal spectaculars, this being the Scaun on the north coast. On the horizontal rock platform to the right of the arch, a colony of shags passes the time of day.

Inset: gannets are also plentiful around Westray. The fortunate will see them diving for fish, but even when passing by in level flight they are perhaps the most impressive of Orkney's seabirds.

74 Pierowall is Westray's main village, seen here from the north with another of those lovely beaches and clear green water enhancing the view. Beyond is Fitty Hill, highest point on Westray.

Left: Westray's Noup Head is famous for these sheer cliffs and its lighthouse. Right: but it is best known for its huge seabird colonies – note the fluffy young gannet at the top of the picture.

76 Going from Westray to Papa Westray gives travellers the chance to sample the world's shortest scheduled flight, just two minutes for the two-mile hop. This plane is touching down at Papa Westray.

This complex of agricultural buildings is Holland Farm which includes the Bothy Museum of local artefacts. Inset: one of the more interesting retired vehicles on the islands. Rust in peace!

78 West of Holland Farm is the Knap of Howar, probably the oldest standing stone houses in Europe at over 5,000 years old. Fascinating items have survived, such as the grindstone in the inset picture.

North Ronaldsay is the most remote of all the Orkney Isles. Its sheep are an ancient breed which are kept on the foreshore by a stone dyke and live mainly on seaweed. Inset: ringed plover.

80 Left: first lit in 1789, North Ronaldsay's old lighthouse only remained in use until 1809.
Right: the new one was built in the 1850s and is the tallest land-based lighthouse in the British Isles.

Left: at the south end of the island is North Ronaldsay Bird Observatory. Right: also in the south of **81** the isle, this standing stone is unusual as it is pierced by a small hole, just visible near the centre.

82 Now we turn our attention to southern Orkney. During World War Two, Italian prisoners of war were sent to Orkney and converted two Nissen huts into what we now know as the Italian Chapel.

Mercifully, the exquisite chapel avoided demolition at the end of the war and has become one of **83** Orkney's most treasured sights, positioned on the tiny island of Lamb's Holm, just off Mainland.

84 This aerial view shows Churchill Barriers nos.1-3, connecting, from left, Burray, Glimp's Holm and Lamb's Holm to Mainland. They were built to prevent submarines from entering Scapa Flow

and were topped with 300,000 tons of concrete blocks which can clearly be seen here at Barrier 85
No.3. Before they were built, 'blockships' were sunk with the same aim, but they could be bypassed.

86 The timeless harbour village of St Margaret's Hope occupies a bay on the north coast of South Ronaldsay. The village is probably named after St Margaret, wife of King Malcolm III.

Not the prettiest of sights, but WW2 defence installations like these at Hoxa Head, South Ronaldsay, are such a feature of the Orkney landscape that they deserve illustration.

87

88 Clockwise from top left: model of a Bronze Age burnt mound at Tomb of the Eagles visitor centre; Orphir's unique round church; three of Orkney's 100,000 cattle; Wideford Hill chambered cairn.

This panoramic view across Scapa Flow looks west towards the hills of Hoy (the name simply means **89** 'high'), including Ward Hill, the highest point in Orkney at 481m/1578ft.

90 Left: at the southern end of Hoy a causeway connects to South Walls where this 1813-built Martello Tower is a relic of the Napoleonic wars. Right: memorial to the Longhope lifeboat disaster of 1969.

Scapa Flow Visitor Centre & Museum at Lyness on Hoy tells the story of this huge wartime naval **91** base, in which displays like the one above add atmosphere to these events.

92 In contrast to the other side of the island, Hoy's east coast has several delightful bays like this one, made even more appealing when the heather is in bloom.

Sailing along Hoy's west coast provides a unique opportunity to appreciate the 'architecture' **93** of these splendid cliffs, so many of which are eroded at their base, like this one.

94 After heavy rain, temporary waterfalls appear that plunge straight down the cliffs to the shore, a sight best appreciated from the sea.

Journey's end, as we return to where we started from for a different perspective on the Old Man **95**
of Hoy: this view gives a sense of scale thanks to the tiny figures on the cliff-top to the right.

Published 2014 by Ness Publishing, 47 Academy Street, Elgin, Moray, IV30 1LR
Phone/fax 01343 549663   www.nesspublishing.co.uk

All photographs © Colin and Eithne Nutt except p.13 © Doug Houghton; p.19 Adam Stanford © Aerial-Cam Ltd 2012;
pp.34, 39, 54, 80 (left), 81 (left) & 89 © Paul Turner; p.69 © Allan Welsh; p.82 © Steve Regis

Text © Colin Nutt
ISBN 978-1-906549-26-8

Front cover: Ring of Brodgar; p.1: Norse runic graffiti inside Maeshowe; p.4: Statue of St Olaf in St Magnus Cathedral; this
page: the ferry *Hamnavoe* berthed at Stromness; back cover: Rousay from northern isles ferry

For a list of websites and phone numbers please turn over > > > >

Websites and phone numbers (where available) of featured places in alphabetical order:

Balfour Castle, Shapinsay: www.balfourcastle.co.uk (T) 01856 711 282
Barnhouse Village: www.orkneyjar.com/history/barnhouse
Broch of Gurness: www.historic-scotland.gov.uk (T) 01856 751414
Brough of Birsay: www.historic-scotland.gov.uk (T) 01856 841815
Corrigall Farm Museum: www.orkney.gov.uk (T) 01856 771411
Earl's Palace, Birsay: www.historic-scotland.gov.uk (T) 01856 841815
Eday: www.visiteday.com (T) 01857 622262
Highland Park Distillery: www.highlandpark.co.uk (T) 01856 874619
Hoy: www.hoyorkney.com
Italian Chapel: www.orkneycommunities.co.uk/italianchapel
Kirbister Farm Museum: www.orkney.gov.uk (T) 01856 771411
Kirkwall: www.visitorkney.com/kirkwall
Knap of Howar: www.historic-scotland.gov.uk (T) 01856 872044
Maeshowe: www.historic-scotland.gov.uk (T) 01856 761606
Midhowe Broch: www.historic-scotland.gov.uk (T) 01856 841815
Midhowe Chambered Cairn: www.historic-scotland.gov.uk (T) 01856 841815
Ness of Brodgar: www.orkney.uhi.ac.uk (T) 01856 569000
Noltland Castle: www.historic-scotland.gov.uk (T) 01856 841815
North Link Ferries: www.northlinkferries.co.uk (T) 0845 6000 449
North Ronaldsay: www.visitorkney.com/northronaldsay
North Ronaldsay Bird Observatory: www.nrbo.co.uk (T) 01857 633200
Orkney: www.visitorkney.com
Orkney Inter-Island Ferries: www.orkneyferries.co.uk (T) 01856 872044
Orkney Museum, Kirkwall: www.orkney.com/museums (T) 01856 771411
Quoyness Chambered Cairn: www.historic-scotland.gov.uk (T) 01856 841815